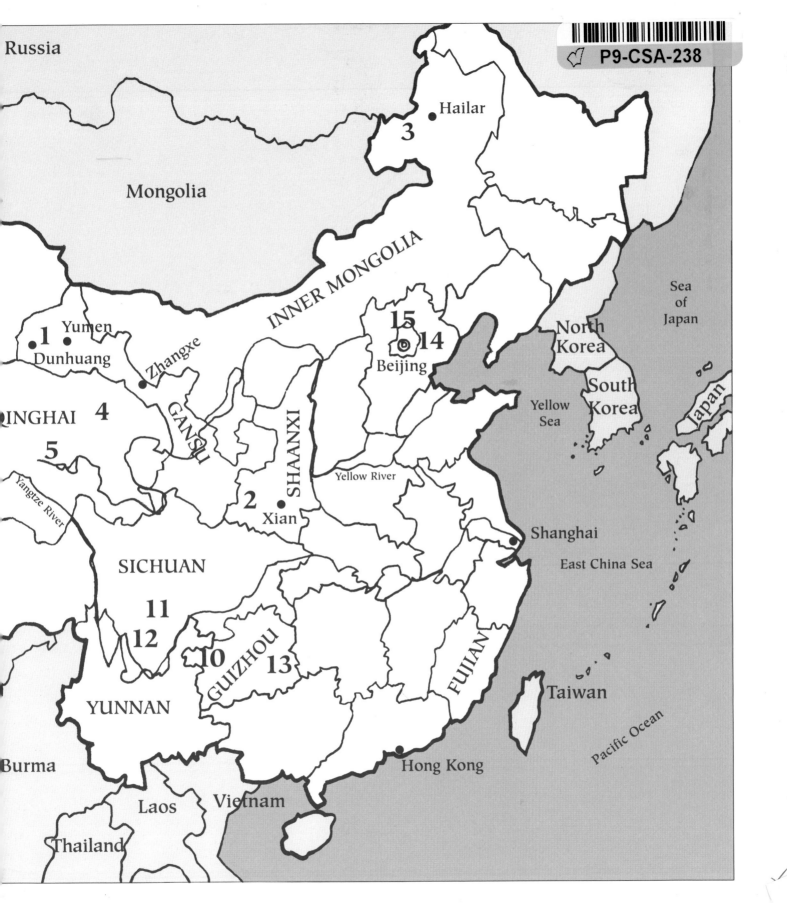

THE CHILDREN OF CHINA

Also by Song Nan Zhang: *A Little Tiger in the Chinese Night: an autobiography in art*
Five Heavenly Emperors: Chinese Myths of Creation

I would like to express my heartfelt appreciation to those who have loved and supported my art through the years.

With additional translations from Chinese to English by Hao Yu Zhang

Published in Canada by Tundra Books, Montreal, Quebec H3Z 2N2
Published in the United States by Tundra Books of Northern New York, Plattsburgh, N.Y. 12901
Library of Congress Catalog Number 95-60981

Canadian Cataloging in Publication Data:

Zhang, Song Nan, 1943-
      The Children of China
ISBN 0-88776-363-4

1. Children — China — Juvenile literature. 2. Minorities — China — Juvenile literature. 3. China — Description and travel — Juvenile literature. I. Title.

DS779.23.Z47   1995   j951.05'9'089   C95-900425-4

The publisher has applied funds from its Canada Council block grant for 1995 toward the editing and production of this book.

The publisher wishes to acknowledge the assistance of France Pepper.

The publisher thanks the following individuals for graciously lending their paintings for the production of this book: Adam Balinsky and Tracey Aaron, Mr. and Mrs. B. Berman, Mr. and Mrs. D. Granofsky, M. and Mme. G. Gravel, Mme. Louise Joubert, Mr. and Mrs. C. Pourtous, Mr. and Mrs. J.K. Sproule, Mitchell Tessler, Mrs. Zanobia Man Kin Wong.

Printed in Hong Kong by South China Printing Co. Ltd.

THE CHILDREN OF CHINA

An Artist's Journey

SONG NAN ZHANG

TUNDRA BOOKS

Our son takes his first steps in a troubling time in China. Would the Buddha protect him from fear?

Beginnings

Nearly everyone who looks at these paintings remarks on how colorful they are, how romantic the subject, how happy the people. Can anyone in the world be that joyful?

My answer is: "To me, they were." It is how I saw them, sketched them, photographed them, remembered them, and even, as I painted them later, imagined them. To me, they represented freedom in a country without freedom, the right to live one's own way, to dress, work, worship and bring up children according to ancient customs.

China had just been through ten horrifying years. From 1966 when Chairman Mao Tse-tung announced the Cultural Revolution until his death in 1976, no one was safe. Innocent people were marched through the streets, beaten, tried in public squares and sent away to be "reeducated." My father, my brother and my sisters were banished to hard labor in the far ends of China and would not see each other for seven years. My mother became so ill from being visited and threatened, then from losing her home and family, that she had a breakdown and would be an invalid for the rest of her life. I was the luckiest because my "reeducation" took place on farms near Beijing.

During those frightening years, no one in the cities of China wanted to stand out in any way. To draw attention to yourself was to invite suspicion. You dressed in dark grays, browns, blacks and blues. You lived in crowded compounds, three generations often confined to a single room, with the stench from garbage and human excrement everywhere.

Can you imagine then how the nomadic people of China seemed to me, roaming open spaces, dressing in glorious colors, living free? One could not hope of ever being allowed outside China. That would be like hoping to visit another planet. But these people lived within the Chinese borders. I had hopes that I might one day visit them. As soon as the terror ended and the new premier announced an end to chaos, and I was given back my job teaching at the art institute, I used all my holidays to travel and visit these peoples I had dreamed of knowing.

My first son was born in Beijing in 1970, at the the height of the Cultural Revolution and the terror. What would China be like when he grew up? My father used to quote an old Chinese saying: "A child won't know how much love his parents have given him until he becomes one, too."

We named our son Hao Yu, meaning "the bright universe," and we gave him so much love. One day we took him to the Sun Temple Park near the compound where we lived. There, with his mother's help, he walked his first step. I was very proud and excited as I took his photograph. More than twenty years have passed, yet I still like to look at the photo.

I have painted that first step not in the park but in front of a mural from the Dunhuang caves. They lie far to the west of Beijing on the Silk Road that traders traveled to reach China 2,500 years ago. The mural shows the Buddha holding up his hand to dispel fear.

So many nationalities passed along the Silk Road over the centuries, so many generations of artists and artisans worked on the murals and reliefs, that their work seemed an example of the continuity of life through art — just as a child is the continuity of life.

I start, too, with a baby from another culture. This Hui baby was born in the year of the tiger. That's his animal sign, so he is nicknamed Tiger, given a tiger hat, shirt, shoes and tiger toys.

How did the custom start? I was taught that when the Buddha was dying, he called all the animals to him. Only twelve came: a horse, snake, dragon, rabbit, tiger, buffalo, rat, pig, dog, rooster, monkey and goat. To reward them, the Buddha made each one the symbol of a year. Every twelve years the same animal sign returns.

Many Chinese — not just Buddhists — can tell you their animal sign. The Hui minority are Muslim; they do not eat pork and avoid the word "pig." If this Hui baby had been born in the year of the pig, he would have been given the color sign of black instead of an animal sign.

These paintings of two different babies seemed a good way to begin looking at children who still strike me as so beautiful and confident in their innocence.

This Hui baby was born in the year of the tiger, so he is surrounded by tigers. Can you count them?

Mongolian chess

I like this painting of a boy playing chess with his grandfather on the grasslands of Mongolia because it is so peaceful. Sheep quietly graze in the background. Passing clouds cast their shadows in the lake.

The scene is the opposite of what most people think of when they hear the word "Mongolian." They think of Genghis Khan and his ruthless army of horseback warriors sweeping across Asia, destroying any who opposed them. When Marco Polo visited China and met Kublai Khan, the grandson of Genghis, Mongolia was one of the most powerful nations in the world.

While history leaves the impression that Mongolians are a violent people, if you visit Inner Mongolia, whether invited or not, you will be welcomed as a friend.

Most Mongolians still live the nomadic life of their ancestors. They prize horses. Legend says the first Mongolian was born on the back of a horse. Babies who can barely open their eyes are tied to their mother's back as she rides. Five- or six-year-olds are already veteran riders.

Once a year, in late summer or early fall, Mongolians from all over the grasslands gather for their biggest festival — the Nadam. People use the off-season to stage games like polo, horse racing, wrestling, archery or just to sing, dance and have fun. These games give people a glimpse of what the ancient warriors may have looked like.

Once a year Mongolians also hold memorial ceremonies at the Mausoleum of Genghis Khan in Ordeos on Gandeer Hill. Mongolians see him as their national hero, but today they pray for eternal peace and prosperity, not war and glory.

Incidentally, Mongolian chess is almost the same as European chess; though the King is called Khan, the Queen is called a Tigress or a Lioness, and the knights are on camels.

A Mongolian shepherd takes the time to play chess with his grandson in this peaceful mountain setting.

In the blustery cold, a Tibetan mother rides through falling snow, holding her children close to her.

Safe and warm with Mother

Western children would like many things about the family life of the Tibetans who live on a high plateau near the Himalayan Mountains. It can get very cold there, but no matter how biting the weather, small children are never cold. A Tibetan mother — like the one I have painted — carries her young ones with her, on her back or against her bosom, bundled up and protected.

Western children who like to crawl into bed with their parents would also like Tibetan life where a whole family often sleeps together on one big clay bed. And something else: they rarely wash or undress because of the dry cold.

Until recently, some Tibetan children didn't even have to go to school. They traveled with their families all year, as the animal herds were led to greener pastures. But now many herders send their children to school in Lhasa, the capital of Tibet, and leave them there in dormitories during the summer migrations. These children may not see their parents from early spring until they return with the first snowfall.

The Tibetan people who live in the northwest part of China believe their people are as old as the Himalayas and the Yarlung River. According to legend, a celestial monkey once lived on top of the Gonggar Mountains and looked down to where two great rivers, the Yarlung and the Yarlung Tsangpo, meet. One day a beautiful girl appeared in the river. She fell in love with the monkey. The two married and had many children. Their descendants became the first generation of Tibetans. There are two big caves on top of the Gonggar Mountains and people say that is where the girl and the celestial monkey got married.

History tells another story. The first known tribal leader of Tibet actually lived in the Yarlung Valley. His tribe conquered adjacent tribes and intermarried with them. They were the first Tibetans.

A Tibetan family welcome

When I traveled in remote areas of China it was always exhilarating, after days of driving or hiking without seeing any sign of life, to glimpse a tent or a small stone house on the horizon. The people living in them were always warm and friendly; they know how hard it is to travel on the plateau.

The family in this painting live by a small creek in the mountains of Qinghai province that is the source of the Yellow River. They wear long, heavy fur or felt coats all year long. In nice weather, they simply bare one shoulder. They know the treacherous weather on the Tibetan Plateau where temperatures vary so much from morning to evening.

Notice how both men and women braid their hair, mixing in pieces of turquoise, coral and silver. The men sweep the braids over the tops of their heads while the women and girls let the braids fall on their shoulders. The aim is to have 108 braids in the hair. Notice also the cheeks made rosy by the high cold climate.

Although some Tibetans live in brick and stone houses, those who travel with their cattle, sheep and yaks live in tents of a felt made from yak hair. Animals are used in many ways. Clothes, shoes, hats and rugs are made of animal skin. Children's toys are made of sheep bones. Women, as part of the New Year celebration, rinse their faces in milk. Dwellings are heated by burning dried animal manure as fuel.

Tibetans eat a great deal of meat, particularly mutton and beef which they preserve by drying under the fierce highland sun. This "meat-jerky" is the main source of protein during the long and harsh winter. Yak butter is put in tea or combined with barley flour, called *tsampa*, to make dough. It is also used as oil in lamps.

Tibetans are very religious. They practice a form of Buddhism using prayer wheels and make pilgrimages every year to many temples high in the mountains.

Fur is worn all year by this Tibetan family. In warmer weather, they simply bare a shoulder.

Two Kazakh girls ride an ox to get to school while their mother watches from the door of their yurt.

Children along the Silk Road.

The Silk Road is the most romantic part of China, and it was the part of China I most wanted to see, with its vast deserts and mountains and the variety of its people. Ever since Marco Polo passed this way in the 1270s, traveling all the way from Italy to Peking (Beijing), it has been the meeting place for traders from the West and East. Those who have settled there reflect the many peoples who have passed this way through the centuries.

I, of course, reached the Silk Road from the direction opposite Marco Polo's. I came from Beijing, traveling from east to west, and picked up the famous caravan route in the city of Dunhuang, site of the famous caves.

Many semi-nomadic peoples live in western Xinjiang: the Tajiks, the Kazakhs and the Khirgiz. The two young Kazakh girls in my painting are riding an old ox to get to school. Their mother stands at the door of their yurt, watching them leave. The children helped set up the yurt when the family moved to this mountainous area to pasture their animals.

Not so long ago few children of nomadic families went to school. But things are changing. I met a young Khirgiz man in a bus station in Xinjiang who was on his way to Beijing to attend university. He had attended a "traveling" school. Many herding families now hire teachers to travel with them.

Do you like the painting of the little Kazakh girl with the huge sheep? She is looking after them, but it seems the other way round, and these sheep are as gentle and friendly as dogs. Their long, soft hair makes some of the finest wool in the world.

"If you haven't been to Kashgar, you haven't seen Xinjiang," many people told me. It took five days on a bus circling the Taklamakan Desert to reach it. Its shops and open markets don't seem to have closed since Marco Polo arrived. Even the Communists could not stop the trading. The residents are mostly Uygurs; they are Muslim, look European, make superb handicrafts and produce delicious grapes and watermelons on the oases.

I painted this young Uygur girl tending her father's pottery shop because I liked the pensive look on her face, her Uygur outfit of dress over trousers, the bandanna holding back her ponytail, and the pattern of the plates and jars.

Sheep as big as this one can be as gentle as a family dog with children who love to pet them.

A Uygur girl tends a pottery shop in Kashgar. Marco Polo might have witnessed such a scene.

Listening to a hand drum

From Kashgar I traveled south for two days, along a highway near the Pakistani border. I arrived at Tash Qurghan where caravans still stop after crossing the Pamir Mountains. Here they not only trade and rest, but enjoy the unique entertainment of the Tajik people.

There was so much to look at and listen to.

I stood on top of a ruin and watched a sheepherder lead a flock down a mountainside. Here, too, I noticed that sheep are treated like friendly dogs, as part of an extended family. In the West, people think of sheep only as providing wool and meat. But among the Tajiks and other nomadic Chinese, sheep provide milk and butter as well.

I watched and listened to women playing hand drums. Later, as I painted this picture I could still hear the drum beats. The Tajiks are justly famous for their dancing. The women dance to the drums and the men do an eagle dance, imitating the bird's flight. The eagle provides more than inspiration. Flutes are made from its bones.

I also liked the colorful embroidery on the pillbox hats. The women hold these in place with large scarves that flap down their backs.

The Tajiks are of Persian descent and are Muslim. They came over the mountains long ago and stayed on the Chinese side. Some still live in yurts and some have simple brick houses. I peeked into one small house and realized that several generations lived there. I counted ten adults and eight children in a single house.

I enjoyed my few days among the Tajiks very much. To me they were a lesson in how it is possible to be happy without wealth, to spread cheer through music and dancing, even though the work is hard and the climate difficult.

No wonder the caravans loved to stop there.

On the edge of the Pamir Mountains, the Tajiks welcome weary travelers with hand-drum music and dancing.

Even while gathering leaves for fuel, this Yi mother and her children dress beautifully.

The mountain world of the Yi

The first question I am asked by anyone looking at this painting is: "Do these people really dress like that when they're working?" The answer is: "Yes, they do."

This Yi mother in Guizhou province is gathering leaves with her two children. The Yi people live mostly in the mountains — after all, they say, Isn't that where the sun and moon live? They use leaves as fuel for their kitchen fires. The children make a little money collecting and selling the leaves. Like children everywhere, they also have fun playing in them.

I had mixed feelings as I painted this picture for I have my own memories of working in the autumn woods. During the Cultural Revolution, when I was sent to the countryside to be "reeducated," we collected leaves to use as food. In the early 1960s, when famine killed millions of people in China, even leaves became hard to find.

Yi women make their own fabrics and embroider them elaborately. In my painting, I tried to emphasize the warm colors: the mother's reddish-blue dress in contrast with the golden background.

Yi children are said to be as agile as goats. A Yi epic tells of a child who could climb mountains at the age of one, hammer out swords at two and kill a leopard with a deadly punch at three. The girl in my painting was not that agile, but she still seemed able to follow her goats anywhere in the mountains. Her cape is made of a goat wool called *chaerwa*. It is warm and water resistant.

The Yi people in the Liang Mountains of Sichuan hold a torch festival each year on June 24. They stage wrestling matches, horse races, and fights between bulls, between cocks and between goats. Then they bring out yellow parasols. Bright yellow is easily seen from a distance, and when thousands of these parasols are raised, the mountain slopes seem to bloom with yellow flowers. Children love to run through the crowd and hide among the parasols. That is how I painted a young boy. Can you find him?

Later on, after sunset, thousands of torches will be lit to burn all night long. It is indeed a magnificent sight.

This Yi girl is almost as agile in climbing the dangerous mountains as the goats she takes care of.

At the Yi torch festival, yellow parasols blossom like flowers and children run and hide among them.

Bronze and silver

The Miao people wear the most expensive head-dresses and jewelry in all China and some of the most elaborate costumes.

Even the children have beautiful silver to wear on their heads, around their necks and sewn onto their clothes. Needless to say, they wear it only for holidays. Can you imagine wearing it to school?

The jewelry is made with great care. The silver is cut and molded into shapes found in nature: the sun, moon, flowers and butterflies. Some are shaped like dragons and birds.

Girls at the age of twelve or thirteen start to make their wedding clothes. They both weave the fabric and embroider it, often attaching pieces of silver.

The Miao people live in the mountains of the south and have a long history of living independently, fighting anyone who tried to dominate them.

In Miao households, three generations — grandparents, parents and children — live together. You may have noticed that this is common among many minorities that farm or migrate with their animals. But the Miao have many traditions distinctly their own. For instance, boys usually are given names to do with wealth, stones, rocks, dragons, snakes, oxen or horses. Girls, on the other hand, are named after a flower, leaf, vegetable, bird, water, rice or even an insect or worm!

The children are brought up to be extremely polite. They greet a guest, lead him to a seat, and offer tea, holding the cup between two hands like a precious gift.

For this painting of a Miao mother and child wearing their great silver, I chose an ancient bronze background design. It has nothing to do with the Miao people, but I liked the combination of silver representing wealth and bronze standing for power and the idea that art outlives both.

Magnificent silver jewelry is worn on the head, around the neck and sewn on clothes of Miao women and girls.

All over China children enjoy the final day of the New Year celebrations with colorful street fairs.

Here teenagers on stilts wait to compete while boys in Manchu costumes hold signs advertising tea.

The Spring Festival

Most of the people in China are Han. They have inhabited the area for thousands of years, first as tribes and chiefdoms along the Yellow and Yangtze rivers, then as kingdoms, and finally as empires that would become China. The Han are everywhere in China and they are the people one thinks of when they ask: "Are you Chinese?"

But it is not just the Han who have made the Spring Festival the biggest holiday time in the country. The Festival opens the Chinese New Year and the celebrations last fifteen days. The Hui, the Manchu, the Miao and a dozen other minorities take part.

While everyone joins in the party, starting with the family dinner on New Year's Eve, it is the children who enjoy it most. The money gifts they receive from relatives go for cookies, candy, and, best of all, firecrackers. The excitement builds until that final fifteenth day, when it seems to me we always found a way to dress up and have fun.

In city and village, streets come alive with festivals offering folk dancing and folk opera. Children practice all year for the competitions. Who has made the best paper lantern? Who can give the best performance on stilts?

I did this large painting to celebrate the return of color, costumes and individual creativity after the depressing drabness of the Cultural Revolution.

I end this book as I began it, with a memory of my own son as a baby, eager for life, open, unafraid. In keeping with my theme of art and children being the continuity of life, I painted a collection of Chinese art and artifacts around him and me. Many originated with peasants in the countryside: the paper tiger cut-outs, the masks including one from the Peking Opera, the folk toys, and the pottery vases recently found near Banshan after 4,000 years. The paintings on the doors are of fearless warriors who scare off demons, and they are widely reproduced in China. The wooden masks just behind us date from the Stone Age. The names of the artists who created this art are lost in time but we treasure their creations and are grateful.

I hold my son up to the future against a collage of ancient Chinese icons that show how art has endured.

From my father to my sons

My father used to say: "All children are born good."

I, too, believe that children are born good. The children I saw on my travels through China, and later in Europe and North America, confirm it.

My father said he was taught it his first day of school. When he was a boy growing up in Shanghai, long before the war and the Communist Revolution, he went to a traditional Chinese school that concentrated on trying to keep children good.

Artists are like children, as they try to see the world around them with innocent eyes. They make fresh for us what is stale and depressing. An artist searches to understand the magic of the world — just as a baby tries to understand the magic of gravity by dropping a spoon on the floor. The artist shares his sense of magic through the art he gives us. A baby trying and learning gives us the same sense of wonder.

We who wish all people could be as good and innocent as children should wish that everyone might become artists of some kind as they grow up. It is the message I would give my sons. For in the end, out of China's long and troubled history, it is not the empires of the powerful that have survived, but the work of artists done in caves over a thousand years ago.

RELIGION IN CHINA

There are many religions practiced in China but most people are Confucian, Taoist or Buddhist.

Confucianism is based on the teachings of K'ung Fu-tse, known to Westerners as Confucius. He lived in the ancient state of Lu and died around 479 BC. He was a public official who developed a system of morality to bring about peace and order. Confucians believe in maintaining harmonious relationships with others and worshiping ancestors.

Taoism is based on an ancient book written by Lao-Tze. Tao means "the way" and refers to the path that must be taken to live a good life and be harmonious with nature. It is more mystical in nature than Confucianism and offered more of an emotional outlet.

Buddhism came to China from India in the first century AD. and spread across the country. China has many historic Buddhist sites, showing how strong the religion is in China.

Of the minority religions, Islam is the most prominent. In the seventh century, a hundred Muslim traders arrived in China by sea and settled in the port of Quanzhou in Fujian province. Later, Muslims arrived during the Mongol conquests. From bases in northern China, the Mongol forces raced westward as far as the Black Sea and relocated captured Muslims in China. They gradually integrated into the mainstream culture but kept their faith.

The Kazakhs and Tajiks of western China are not ethnically Chinese but are Caucasians, related to the peoples of central Asia. They form the eastern end of a large Islamic region that extends all the way to Turkey.

There are some Christians in China, mainly in port cities. There is even a small group in central China who consider themselves to be Jewish; they are remnants of traders who once traveled the Silk Road. A few minority peoples in China still practice "folk" or animist religions, ancient beliefs that consider everything in the natural world sacred. Most animists live in the mountains of southern China.

THE SILK ROAD AND THE CAVES OF DUNHUANG

Silk was invented in China around 1500 BC. In the fifth century BC, a Greek doctor serving in the Persian Royal Army visited a country in the East named "Seres." "Ser" means silk or silkworm in Greek. The country was China. Between 329 BC and 323 BC, the generals of Alexander the Great almost reached the western boundaries of China and in their wartime journals they mention a "Silk Country." During the Han dynasty (206 BC — AD 220), contacts between China and the West increased. Silk became a highly valued commodity in Europe and Asia Minor. The caravan route which linked China and Asia Minor, and eventually Europe, was named the "Silk Road" by the 19th-century German geologist, F. von Richthofen. The road begins at Chang-an (the modern city of Xian), passes north of the Gobi Desert, goes over the Tianshan Mountains, reaches central Asia and finally Asia Minor, ending in Damascus, Syria. From there, it was a quick journey to Europe. The road was not only a trade link, it was also the route of cultural exchange between the East and the West. Dunhuang was where merchants rested and traded on the road. The earliest Buddhist caves were begun in approximately AD 366. The caves of Dunhuang house art treasures from China proper, western China, India, Persia and central Asia. Today 492 caves remain.

HERDERS AND THEIR ANIMALS

To herds people, their livestock are all they have. The animals are sources of food and clothing, and they are also companions. People in various parts of China tend different types of animals. North of the Yangtze River, it is cattle; south of the river, it is water buffalo. On the Tibetan Plateau, yaks are the main source of protein and furs for people. Horses are also important, especially to the Mongolians. The Yili valley of Xinjiang was once well known for its magnificent horses. They were known as the "celestial breed."

There are fifty-five officially recognized minorities in China. But because the population is constantly changing, the statistics mentioned below are only approximations. China has seen a steady increase in the number of people moving to the cities.

The **Han**

Population: 1.2 billion people are Han
Where: Live in all parts of China
Religion: Confucians, Buddhists and Taoists

The Han are the majority nationality of China. They speak Mandarin and Cantonese and other dialects and comprise one of the world's largest ethnic groups.

The **Hui**

Nine million
Gansu, Ningxia, Qinghai, Shaanxi, Sichuan, Xinjiang, Yunnan
Muslims

The Hui are closely related to the Han. They speak Mandarin and look and dress like the Han. But they have retained their belief in Islam and observe its customs and traditions. They are the largest religious minority in China outside the Confucian/Taoist/Buddhist mainstream.

The **Miao**

Seven million
Guangxi, Guizhou, Hubei, Hunan, Yunnan
folk/animist religions

The Miao are agriculturalists living primarily in southern China. Some Miao live in Thailand and Laos, where they are known as the Hmong.

The **Uygur**

Seven million
Hunan, Xinjiang Autonomous Region
Muslims

The Uygur people are closely related to the Turks and other central Asian groups. Their language is similar to Turkish and their script is Arabic. They are mainly agricultural people, known through history as able gardeners.

The **Yi**

Seven million
Guangxi, Guizhou, Sichuan, Yunnan
Confucians, Taoists and Buddhists

The Yi are mainly farmers and herders. The women are known for the beautiful embroidery on their clothing.

The **Mongolians**

Five million
Inner Mongolian Autonomous Region
Buddhists

The Mongolians remain a people on horseback and are pastoral, usually living as herders or farmers. Many live in yurts, which are like large, circular tents that can be transported on horseback. Mongolians love to play chess and their national sport is wrestling.

The **Tibetans**

Five million
Gansu, Qinghai, Sichuan, Tibet, Yunnan
Tibetan Buddhists

The Tibetans are a very religious people and some await the day their spiritual leader — the Dalai Lama — returns to his palace in the capital, Lhasa, from exile in northern India.

The **Kazakh**

One million
Qinghai, Xinjiang
Muslims

The Kazakh are related to the people who inhabit Kazakhstan, one of the former Soviet republics. They are semi-nomadic, living in yurts in the spring and summer.

The **Tajik**

Forty thousand
southern Xinjiang
Shiite Muslims

The Tajik are a semi-nomadic people. In the winter, they live in stone houses. They live in yurts as well and are related to the citizens of Tajikistan, a country in central Asia.

j915.105
ZHA

Zhang, Song Nan

The children of
China

$17.95

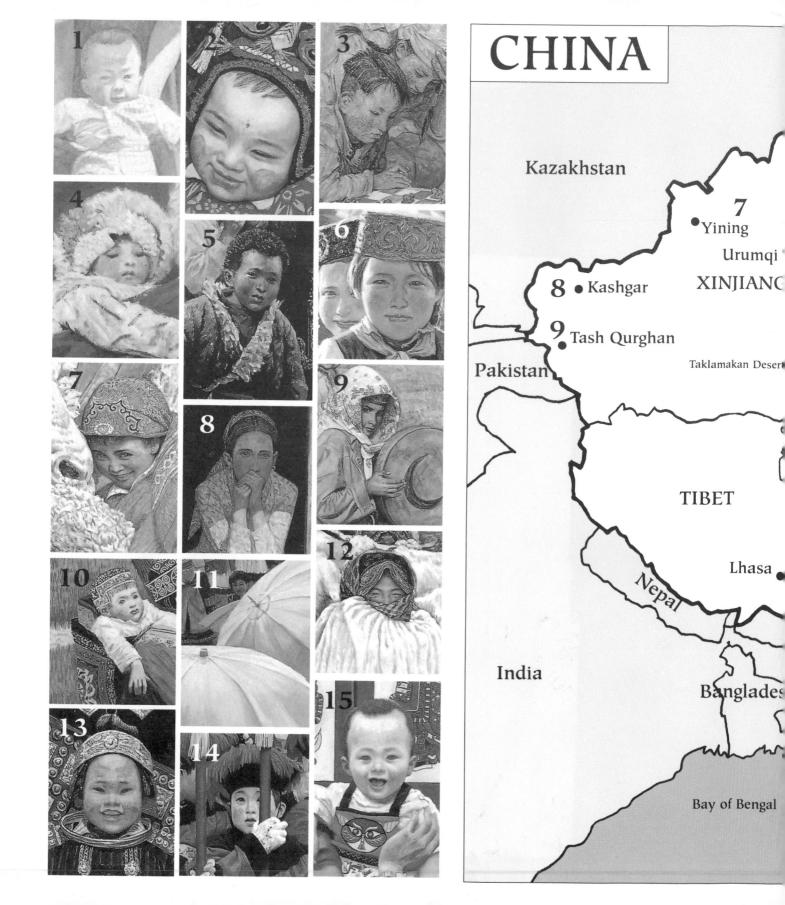

CHINA

Kazakhstan

7
• Yining

Urumqi

XINJIANG

8 • Kashgar

9 • Tash Qurghan

Pakistan

Taklamakan Desert

TIBET

Lhasa •

Nepal

India

Bangladesh

Bay of Bengal